Baseball
Stars

TRIUMPH
BOOKS

This book is available in quantity at special discounts for your group or organization.
For further information, contact:

Triumph Books LLC
814 North Franklin Street
Chicago, Illinois 60610
(312) 337-0747

www.triumphbooks.com

Printed in U.S.A.
ISBN: 978-1-62937-382-9

Content developed & packaged by Alex Lubertozzi

Photos courtesy of AP Images

Contents

Washington Nationals right fielder and 2015 NL MVP Bryce Harper

> "Mike Trout is unbelievable. He's one of the best players in baseball right now, if not the best."
>
> —2015 NL MVP Bryce Harper

#27

Mike Trout

Hometown: Vineland, New Jersey

Team:
Los Angeles Angels of Anaheim

Full name: Michael Nelson Trout

Ht: 6'2" • **Wt:** 235

DOB: August 7, 1991

Position: Center field

2016 Salary: $16,083,000

Bats/Throws: Right/Right

Fast stat: *100* — At 23 years and 253 days old, Mike became the youngest player to reach 100 HRs and 100 SBs, beating Alex Rodriguez by 56 days.

Twitter: @MikeTrout

Did you know? Mike's dad was drafted in the fifth round by the Minnesota Twins in 1983.

As a kid: Mike was an athletic kid and idolized well-rounded players. His favorite player was Yankees shortstop Derek Jeter.

Interesting tidbit: Mike models his game and professional habits after George Brett, a player he thought always did things the "right way."

Fun fact: Mike is the first player in MLB history to have 30 HRs, 49 SBs, and 129 runs in one season (2012).

Fun fact: From 2012 to 2015, Mike finished every year as the runner-up in AL MVP voting—except 2014, the year he won it.

Favorite music: Mike enjoys listening to country music but likes to have fun with his walk-up music, picking songs like Miley Cyrus'"Party in the USA."

Regarded as one of the top two or three position players in the majors since his rookie year of 2012, Mike Trout has few offensive peers in baseball. In four-plus seasons of major league ball, he's already amassed 151 home runs and 437 RBIs with a .305 lifetime batting average. As if that weren't enough, he's a sterling defensive center fielder and a prodigious base-stealer. He had the best WAR (wins-above-replacement) of any position player in either league in 2012, 2013, and 2014, finishing second to the Nationals' Bryce Harper in 2015, and has won a slew of awards in his short career, capped by the AL Most Valuable Player award in 2014.

Chosen by the Angels with the 25th pick in the first round of the 2009 draft, Trout quickly lived up to his promise, earning Minor League Player of the Year honors in 2010. Called up to the big leagues from the Double A team in July 2011, Trout appeared in 40 games but started 2012 down in Triple A. That didn't last long, however. Brought up at the end of April to replace a struggling Bobby Abreu, Trout clicked immediately and has never looked back.

He began making impressive catches in the outfield and making noise with his bat, regularly recording three- and four-hit games. When he scored a run in 14 straight games in July and was named AL Player of the Month, it was clear that Trout was playing some of the best baseball in the majors. He finished his first full season with 30 home runs and 49 stolen bases, the first rookie ever to reach the 30/40 plateau of at least 30 homers and 40 steals. He not only was the unanimous choice for Rookie of the Year, he finished second in the MVP voting to the Tigers' Miguel Cabrera.

Known for his hard work and infectious enthusiasm, Trout has become a fan favorite in Southern California and has earned comparisons to Hall of Famer Mickey Mantle. Whether hitting his own prodigious slams or robbing opposing players of home runs, Trout is one of the best and most exciting players to watch—and at 25, he's just getting started.

#49

Jake Arrieta

Hometown: Plano, Texas

Team: Chicago Cubs

Full name: Jacob Joseph Arrieta

Ht: 6'4" • **Wt:** 225

DOB: March 4, 1986

Position: Pitcher

2016 Salary: $10,700,00

Bats/Throws: Right/Right

Fast stat: 20 — Jake's consecutive-win streak from August 4, 2015, to May 25, 2016, third-best in MLB history since 1913.

Twitter: @JArrieta34

Did you know? Jake pitched for the U.S. national team and started against China in the 2008 Summer Olympics, where he struck out seven over six innings in Team USA's 9–1 victory.

As a kid: Growing up in Texas and idolizing Nolan Ryan, Jake followed the Rangers, but also liked the Seattle Mariners, who had Randy Johnson and other great players in the 1990s.

Favorite foods: Jake's workout regimen extends to his diet—where he incorporates kale juice, fruit, nuts, lean chicken, and seafood to maintain his health and fitness.

Fun fact: The toughest hitter he's faced is Miguel Cabrera. "It doesn't matter what the scouting report says," Jake said, "he can hit it."

Favorite music: Eclectic, depending on his mood and circumstances—soothing, tropical music for the beach, classic rock and alternative before a start.

After three-and-a-half seasons with the Baltimore Orioles, Jake Arrieta was a sub-.500 pitcher with a lifetime ERA of 5.46. Deciding to cut their losses, the Orioles traded Arrieta and reliever Pedro Strop to the Chicago Cubs for a journeyman starting pitcher and a reserve infielder midway through the 2013 season. Arrieta, a starter who'd always had great stuff but couldn't quite figure it out at the big-league level would soon figure it out—with a vengeance.

Finishing 2013 strong with a 4–2 record in nine starts and a 3.66 ERA, Arrieta would become one of the bright spots on a struggling young Cubs team the following season. In 2014 he went 10–5 and posted a career-best 2.53 ERA for a squad that won only 73 games. But it was all prologue to an extraordinary 2015 season that would see Arrieta win the Cy Young Award and rewrite the record book while leading the Cubs to 97 victories and a wild-card berth.

After the 2015 All-Star break, Arrieta went 12–1 in 15 starts (his only loss came when the Phillies' Cole Hamels no-hit the Cubs) with a 0.75 ERA, to bring his season totals to 22–6 and 1.77. He was the NL Pitcher of the Month for both August (6–0) and September (4–0), and on August 30, he pitched his first no-hitter, a 2–0 win against the Dodgers at Dodger Stadium on national TV. Then in October he pitched a five-hit, complete-game shutout against the Pirates in the wild-card playoff game to send the Cubs to the NLDS.

Arrieta, who throws five pitches, including a nasty 95 mph fastball and wicked slider, is known as a workout freak and can be seen doing pushups in the outfield before a start. He's begun 2016 picking up where he left off in 2015, going 9–0 with a 1.56 ERA to help the Cubs to the best record in baseball through May. To top if off, on April 21, 2016, Arrieta pitched the second no-hitter of his career—and second in 11 regular-season starts—a 16–0 win over the Reds in Cincinnati. Having found his inner Sandy Koufax, the only question now is, how long can he keep this up?

BASEBALL STARS

"Josh Donaldson, without a doubt, is the best third baseman in the world."
—hockey/sports commentator Don Cherry

#20

Josh Donaldson

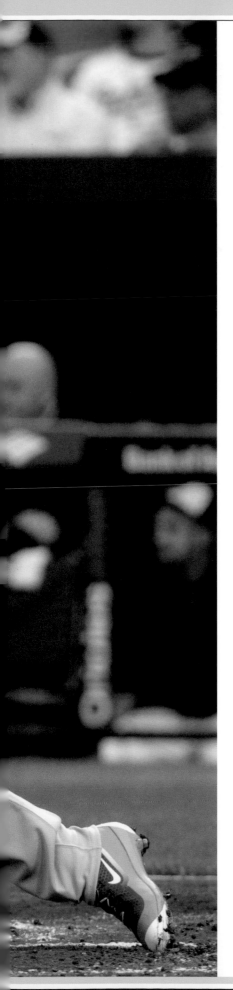

Hometown: Pensacola, Florida

Team: Toronto Blue Jays

Full name: Joshua Adam Donaldson

Ht: 6'1" • **Wt:** 210

DOB: December 8, 1985

Position: Third base

2016 Salary: $11,650,000

Bats/Throws: Right/Right

Fast stat: *84* — League-leading number of extra-base hits Josh bagged in his MVP year of 2015.

Twitter: @BringerOfRain20

Did you know? Josh made a cameo appearance on the History Channel dramatic series *Vikings* on February 18, 2016, playing a Viking warrior named Hoskuld. With his beard and mohawk, he fit right in on set.

As a kid: Josh told his teachers, "Hey, save my signature, because it's gonna be worth something someday." At the time, he was only kidding.

Interesting tidbit: When Josh was 18 months old, he appeared on a local TV station in Florida showing off his "picture perfect" golf swing. He remains an avid golfer to this day.

Fun fact: Josh led the major leagues in voting for the 2015 All-Star Game, shattering the previous record and receiving more than 14 million votes for his second start at third base.

Fun fact: Josh's first hit in the major leagues was a two-run home run for the A's vs. the Blue Jays in 2010.

Favorite music: Hip-hop and reggae.

The reigning American League MVP, Josh Donaldson has quickly become one of the best third basemen in the majors and one of the league's most popular players overall.

Born and raised in Florida by his mother, Lisa French, after his father was sent to prison when he was only five, Josh was a natural athlete, excelling at baseball from the first time his Uncle Chuck tossed him a ball and saw it sail back past his head. Josh's childhood revolved around sports, and his mother supported him as long as he earned A's and B's in school.

When Donaldson was forced to endure taunts from jealous teammates at his high school in Pace, Florida, however, his mother transferred him to Faith Academy in Mobile, Alabama, where he thrived, becoming the Alabama Gatorade Player of the Year his senior season in 2005. He then attended Auburn University, where he shined as a third baseman and first learned to play catcher.

Drafted out of college in 2007 by the Chicago Cubs, he spent two seasons in the Cubs' system before being traded to Oakland, where he worked his way up to a shot at the majors in 2010. It was short-lived, however, as he went 5-for-34 in his first call-up to the big leagues. After spending 2011 in Triple A and converting back to third base, Donaldson started 2012 in Oakland. He shuttled back and forth between the majors and Triple A that season but finished in Oakland, helping the A's to a division title. By 2013 he was the A's regular third baseman and, in his first full season, hit .301 with 24 homers and 93 RBIs, finishing fourth in MVP voting. Though his average dipped to .255 in 2014, his home runs and RBIs went up.

Traded to Toronto after the season, he had his best year in 2015, leading the league in RBIs (123), runs (122), and total bases (352), while hitting .297 with a career-high 41 homers. He helped lead the Blue Jays to the playoffs, where they won the ALDS before falling in six games in the ALCS to the eventual world champion Kansas City Royals.

#34

Bryce Harper

Hometown: Las Vegas, Nevada

Team: Washington Nationals

Full name: Bryce Aron Max Harper

Ht: 6'3" • **Wt:** 215

DOB: October 16, 1992

Position: Right field

2016 Salary: $5,000,000

Bats/Throws: Left/Right

Fast stat: 17 — Bryce finished high school after his sophomore year and began to play college baseball at the age of 17.

Twitter: @Bharper3407

Did you know? Bryce wears the number 34 in honor of Mickey Mantle. The numbers add up to Mantle's jersey number, 7.

As a kid: Bryce's entire life revolved around baseball when he was a kid. He could swing a bat almost from the time he could walk.

Interesting tidbit: Bryce's brother, Bryan, was drafted by the Nats in 2011.

Fun fact: The year Bryce made his major league debut, he became the youngest person to appear in the majors since 2005.

Fun fact: On May 8, 2016, Bryce reached base seven times without an at-bat against the Chicago Cubs (six walks and one hit-by-pitch), the first time a player had done that in 100 years. For the four-game series, he was walked 13 times, a record.

Favorite music: Bryce enjoys current rap music and also likes classic rock.

Bryce Harper became the No. 1 overall pick in the 2010 amateur draft at the age of 17. He debuted in 2012 at the age of 19, and by 2015, at the ripe old age of 22, he collected the first of what promises to be a slew of MVP awards.

Growing up in Las Vegas, Harper's talent as a hitter was obvious to everyone from early on. With prodigious talent beyond his years, he left high school after his sophomore year, earning his GED so he could move on to college and better prepare himself for professional baseball. He played for a community college team and started at the age of 17, impressing against much older players. Already a big-name prospect, his 31 homers in 66 games made him the most highly touted amateur player in years. It was a no-brainer when the Washington Nationals selected him first overall, putting Harper into a system that also included pitching phenom Stephen Strasburg. Though Harper was initially a catcher, he was moved to the outfield in an effort to speed up his development.

Starting the 2012 season in Triple A, Harper was soon called up to the Nationals' big-league club and excelled from the start, hitting a double and collecting an RBI in his first game. He was named Rookie of the Month for May, hitting his first home run and once famously stealing home. Named to his first All-Star Game as a replacement for Giancarlo Stanton, Harper was named Rookie of the Year while helping the Nats to a division title.

Though injuries limited him to just over 100 games in both 2013 and 2014, he was voted to the All-Star Game in 2013 and continued to put up big numbers. But 2015 would be his breakout year. With a slash line of .330/.460/.649, Harper finished the season a close second for the batting title while leading the NL in on-base percentage and slugging. He also led the league in homers (42) and runs scored (118), making his 2015 season one of the most dominant offensive performances in recent memory.

#24

David Price

Hometown: Murfreesboro, Tennessee

Team: Boston Red Sox

Full name: David Taylor Price

Ht: 6'5" • **Wt:** 215

DOB: August 26, 1985

Position: Pitcher

Salary: $30,000,000

Bats/Throws: Left/Left

Fast stat: $5.6 million — When Price was drafted first overall in 2007, he was given what was—at the time—the second largest rookie signing bonus in baseball history.

Twitter: @DAVIDprice24

Did you know? The first hit that Price gave up in the majors was a home run to Derek Jeter.

As a kid: David once nearly quit baseball to go and work at a fast food restaurant.

Favorite foods/fun tidbit: David loves to eat bacon, and his French bulldog, Astro, is also a fan.

Fun fact: David is well-known for his fast pace on the mound, generally taking only five to seven seconds to pitch after he gets the ball from the catcher.

Fun fact: Price led the American League in starts (34), innings pitched (248⅓), and strikeouts (271) in 2014.

Favorite music: David enjoys rap and electronic music.

When the Boston Red Sox signed David Price to a seven-year, $217 million deal in December 2015—cementing their rotation with the No. 1 starter they sorely lacked—the team made Price the highest-paid pitcher in the history of the game. Price, who had just come off a season split between the Tigers and Blue Jays in which he went 18–5 with a league-leading 2.45 ERA, has a lifetime record of 110–57 with a 3.18 ERA. Just 30, the five-time All-Star has already logged eight-plus years of major league service, all of it at an elite level.

The first overall draft pick by Tampa Bay in 2007, Price got the call to the big leagues in September 2008. The surprising Rays worked their way into the playoffs that year and slotted their young hurler in the bullpen. He came through with a memorable save in Game 7 of the ALCS, helping to knock out the defending champion Red Sox and send the Rays to the World Series for the first time. Though the Rays fell short of winning it all, Price picked up another save in Game 2 against the Philadelphia Phillies.

With so much early experience, Price made a smooth transition to full-time starter in 2009, making 23 starts in his first full season and going 10–7. In 2010 Price won 10 games before any other American League pitcher and was named the starting pitcher in the All-Star Game. He finished the year second in the league with 19 wins, a 2.72 ERA, and 188 strikeouts. Then in 2012 he put together his best season, leading the league in wins (20), win-loss percentage (.800), and ERA (2.56) to go with 205 Ks. At the end of the season, he was rewarded with the Cy Young Award.

Price continued to dominate from 2013 to 2015, as he moved from the Rays to the Tigers and then the Blue Jays. If there's any knock against him, it comes from his 0–7 record and 5.30 ERA as a starter in the postseason. Price remains confident, however, saying, "I was just saving all my postseason wins for the Red Sox." With the pitcher and team off to a hot start in 2016, the Red Sox are wagering he's right.

#44

"He's Jesus Christ in a baseball uniform."
—former All-Star first baseman Mark Grace

Paul Goldschmidt

Hometown: The Woodlands, Texas

Team: Arizona Diamondbacks

Full name:
Paul Edward Goldschmidt

Ht: 6'3" · **Wt:** 225

DOB: September 10, 1987

Position: First base

2016 Salary: $5,875,000

Bats/Throws: Right/Right

Fast stat: *124* — Paul's home run total after nearly five full seasons puts him sixth on the Diamondbacks all-time leaderboard.

Did you know? A student-athlete at Texas State University, Paul became the first Bobcats' position player to play in the major leagues.

As a kid: Paul went unrecruited as a baseball player out of high school.

Interesting tidbit: Paul met his future wife, Amy, as a freshman at Texas State. They married in October 2010 and welcomed a son, Jake, into the family in September 2015.

Fun fact: Paul led the National League in intentional walks in both 2013 and 2015, with 19 and 29, respectively.

Fun fact: Despite his exceptional offense and defense, Paul is the fourth-highest-paid player on his team and the 23rd-highest-paid first baseman in the majors.

Favorite music: Country—he changed his walk-up music in 2014 to "It'z Just What We Do" by Florida Georgia Line to break out of a slump.

Known to teammates and fans as "Goldy," Paul Goldschmidt was no bonus baby coming out of Texas State University, despite an impressive collegiate career. Chosen in the eighth round of the 2009 amateur draft by the Arizona Diamondbacks, expectations for Goldy were modest. In time, he would radically change all that.

He excelled in his first year of Rookie ball, then in 2010 was named MVP of the California League as well as the D'backs' Minor League Player of the Year. Moving up to Double A in 2011, he was once again Player of the Year and ticketed for the majors by August.

In his debut on August 1, he collected a hit in his first at-bat and the next day got his first home run as a major leaguer, against the Giants' Tim Lincecum. In his rookie season, he appeared in 48 games, hitting .250 with eight homers and 26 RBIs while helping Arizona to an NL West crown—a solid start, but nothing spectacular. In the NLDS versus Milwaukee, however, Goldschmidt put on a hitting clinic in a losing effort, despite sitting out Game 1 of the five-game series. Goldy hit .438 with six RBIs and two homers, including a grand slam in Game 3—becoming only the third rookie in major league history to hit one in the postseason.

The D'backs' regular first baseman by 2012, Goldy put together an impressive season, hitting .286 with 20 homers and 82 RBIs. He also hit his first two regular-season grand slams within four days of each other in June. His second full-season, 2013, would be his breakout year. He was selected to his first All-Star Game and led the league in home runs (36), RBIs (125), total bases (332), slugging (.551), and OPS (.952), while batting .302. Finishing second in MVP voting to Pittsburgh's Andrew McCutchen, he also collected his first Gold Glove at first base.

In 2015 he was again runner-up in MVP balloting, this time to the Nationals' Bryce Harper, and hit a career-best .321 with 33 homers and 110 RBIs. Adding a second Gold Glove as well, to many he's the finest all-around first baseman in the game.

#13

Salvador Pérez

Hometown: Valencia, Venezuela

Team: Kansas City Royals

Full name:
Salvador Johan Pérez Diaz

Ht: 6'3" • **Wt:** 240

DOB: May 10, 1990

Position: Catcher

2016 Salary: $2,000,000

Bats/Throws: Right/Right

Fast stat: 56% — Through 42 games at catcher in early 2016, Salvy has thrown out 15 of 27 runners (56%) attempting to steal against him.

Twitter: @SalvadorPerez15

Did you know? Salvy hit a home run off 2014 World Series MVP Madison Bumgarner, representing the only run given up by Bumgarner in five World Series appearances covering 36 innings from 2010 to 2014.

As a kid: Salvy's mother, Yilda, would pitch him bottle caps and kernels of corn that Salvy would hit with a broomstick to practice his hitting.

Favorite foods: Salvy loves the cuisine of his home, Venezuela, and frequents Kansas City's Empanada Madness, where he particularly enjoys their shredded beef empanadas.

Fun fact: Salvy played with and against the Houston Astros' second baseman José Altuve, a fellow Venezuelan, while growing up.

Favorite music: Reggaeton—his walk-up music is "50 Sombras de Austin" by Arcángel.

A fter hitting .364 and starting the rally that gave his Royals a lead in the fifth and deciding game of the 2015 World Series, Salvador Pérez became the first catcher to win series MVP honors since 1992, by unanimous vote. A year before, he'd hit .333 with a homer and four RBIs in the World Series, a losing effort in seven games versus the San Francisco Giants.

But Salvy, as fans and teammates know him, has become arguably the best catcher in the game due mostly to his outstanding defense. The three-time All-Star has collected three Gold Gloves in his three full seasons behind the plate for the resurgent Royals. At the same time, he's amassed 71 home runs and 301 RBIs while posting a lifetime average of .278. And his postseason offensive output has been even more impressive: in two playoff runs, Pérez has hit five homers while driving in 14.

Born in Valencia, Venezuela, and raised by his mother and grandmother after his father left, his mother, Yilda, would sell homemade cakes and flan to support the family. But, luckily for Salvy, Venezuela is a baseball-crazy nation (outside of the U.S., only the Dominican Republic has sent more players to the major leagues than Venezuela). So when Salvy's mother enrolled him in a baseball school to give him something to do and keep him away from bad influences, his talents for throwing, catching, and hitting were soon discovered. At eight years old, he decided to become a catcher, and by 14 he knew he wanted to catch at the professional level.

Signed for $65,000 by Kansas City at 16, Pérez started his pro career in the Arizona Rookie League in 2007. In August 2011 he was called up to the majors. In his first game, he picked off two base runners, caught five pop-ups, and banged out his first hit. In 39 games that year, he batted .331 with three homers and 21 RBIs. He was in the big leagues to stay. By 2013 he was the Royals' everyday catcher and a perennial All-Star and Gold Glove catcher. And in 2015, he led Kansas City to its first World Series title in 30 years.

#40

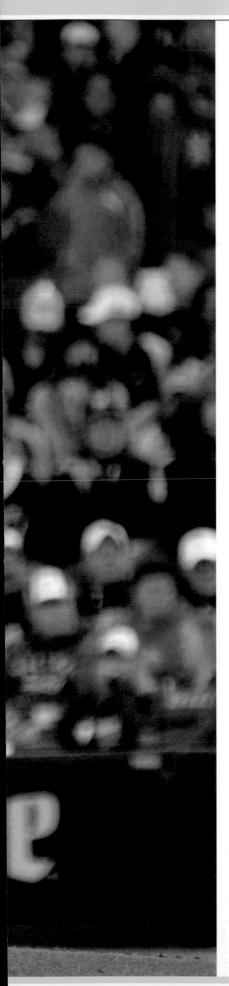

"He's so good at what he does. This guy's one of the best left-handers in the game."

—San Francisco Giants manager Bruce Bochy

Madison Bumgarner

Hometown: Hickory, North Carolina

Team: San Francisco Giants

Full name: Madison Kyle Bumgarner

Ht: 6'5" • **Wt:** 250

DOB: August 1, 1989

Position: Pitcher

2016 Salary: $9,750,000

Bats/Throws: Right/Left

Fast stat: *0.25* — Madison's cumulative ERA over three World Series championship runs with the Giants, covering five appearances and 36 innings pitched.

Did you know? Throwing a ball is the only thing that Madison does left-handed.

As a kid: His childhood home was a log cabin that his father, Kevin, built. Madison slept in the loft.

Interesting tidbit: Madison grew up in a rural area near Hickory, North Carolina, called "Bumtown" due to the abundance of people living there over the years with the last name Bumgarner.

Fun fact: In high school before meeting his future wife, Ali, Madison dated a girl who shared the same name, Madison Bumgarner (no relation).

Fun fact: In addition to winning the 2014 World Series MVP, Madison also won a Silver Slugger award for best-hitting pitcher (he hit .258 with 4 HRs and 15 RBIs) and was named Male Athlete of the Year by AP.

Favorite music: Country rock.

When it comes to World Series heroics, fans may think of home-run hitters like Babe Ruth and Reggie Jackson. But it would be hard to argue that any player has ever surpassed the performance of San Francisco hurler Madison Bumgarner in the Giants' three World Series championships in 2010, 2012, and 2014. In four starts and one relief appearance, he's gone 4–0 while striking out 31 and allowing one lone earned run over 36 innings for an otherworldly ERA of 0.25.

His overall stats in the postseason—a 7–3 record and 2.14 ERA—look positively pedestrian in comparison. In his regular-season career (all spent with the Giants), he's compiled a 91–60 record and a 2.99 ERA, making him one of the most dominant starting pitchers in the game. But as a clutch player on baseball's biggest stage, no one else even comes close.

A teenage phenom, Bumgarner was chosen 10th overall by the Giants in the 2007 amateur draft. He was first called up to the majors in September 2009, starting in place of an injured Tim Lincecum. He didn't record a decision in four appearances but did post a sterling 1.80 ERA. Though he didn't make the Opening Day roster in 2010, he returned to the big leagues in June, this time to stay. In 18 starts, he went 7–6 with a solid 3.00 ERA, helping the Giants to a division title.

But it would be in October when Bumgarner was destined to shine. He went 2–0 with a 2.18 ERA in four appearances in the 2010 postseason, including eight scoreless innings against the Rangers in a pivotal World Series Game 4 victory in Texas. Two years later, he would again allow zero runs over seven innings against the Detroit Tigers in his one World Series start. And in 2014, he would be named World Series MVP, earning two wins and a save, while allowing just one run over 21 innings pitched against Kansas City.

Bumgarner, a three-time All-Star, had his best regular season in 2015, going 18–9 with a 2.93 ERA as the Giants missed the playoffs. Off to a hot start in 2016, no opponent hopes to face him come October.

#19

> *"You look at the pitches he takes. It's crazy. Nasty pitches that he lays off. Real good hitters do that."*
> —Toronto Blue Jays hitting coach Dwayne Murphy

José Bautista

Hometown:
Santo Domingo, Dominican Republic

Team: Toronto Blue Jays

Full name:
José Antonio Bautista Santos

Ht: 6'0" • **Wt:** 205

DOB: October 19, 1980

Position: Right field

2016 Salary: $14,000,000

Bats/Throws: Right/Right

Fast stat: *227* — Home runs hit by José from 2010 to 2015, an average of 37.8 a year and the most of any player in the majors.

Twitter: @JoeyBats19

Did you know? The New York Yankees tried to sign José for $5,000 in 1999. He just laughed.

As a kid: Growing up around his neighborhood in Santo Domingo, José was known to his friends as "El Raton" (the Rat) because he was skinny and had big ears.

Favorite meal for breakfast: An egg white omelet with steak, cheese, onions, peppers, and potato.

Fun fact: José led the majors in walks in 2011 with 132 and the AL in 2015 with 110. From 2010 to 2015, he's had 14 more walks than strikeouts, an unusual feat for a power hitter.

Fun fact: José has always been a gifted student and likes to read, but his favorite subject is math.

Favorite music: Reggaeton, hip-hop, and house music.

When José Bautista began his major league career in 2004, he achieved the dubious distinction of becoming the only player ever to appear on five different rosters—the Orioles, Devil Rays, Royals, Mets, and Pirates—in one season. But for a light-hitting utility infielder/outfielder chosen in the 20th round of the 2000 draft, being traded and moved around by teams was nothing unusual.

After four unremarkable seasons with Pittsburgh and one with Toronto, Bautista adjusted his swing in 2009, seeing immediate results as he hit 10 homers that September. It wasn't a fluke, either. He'd simply transformed himself into one of the most feared power hitters in baseball, almost overnight. In 2010 he led both leagues with 54 home runs, more than triple his previous season high. His 124 RBIs were almost double his career best to that point. In 2011 he hit another 43 homers to lead the majors. From 2010 to 2015, no major league player hit more home runs than Bautista's 227. Add to that his 582 RBIs, a .555 slugging average, and .945 OPS, and it's hard to find a more complete slugger in the game today.

As a young prospect out of the Dominican Republic, scouts recognized Bautista's power potential, but he struggled to sign with a big-league club. Out of high school, he accepted a $300,000 offer from Cincinnati, only to see it rescinded when the Reds changed ownership. He ended up at Chipola College in Florida, where he eventually became a low draft pick of the Pirates. After being tried out at six different positions and as many teams, he's come into his own as a hitter, making six straight All-Star teams since 2010.

In 2015 Bautista played in his first postseason after the Blue Jays won the AL East. In Game 5 of the ALDS versus Texas, Bautista hit a three-run home run to put the Blue Jays up for good and clinch the series. Although the Jays lost to Kansas City in the ALCS, Bautista hit .293 with four homers and 11 RBIs in the playoffs. At 35 Bautista may have been a late bloomer, but he shows no signs of slowing down.

#17

"The sky's the limit for him."
— Chicago Cubs manager Joe Maddon

Kris Bryant

Hometown: Las Vegas, Nevada

Team: Chicago Cubs

Full name: Kristopher Lee Bryant

Ht: 6'5" • **Wt:** 230

DOB: January 4, 1992

Position: Third base/Left field

2016 Salary: $652,000

Bats/Throws: Right/Right

Fast stat: *99* — Kris' RBI total for 2015 was the most by an MLB rookie since Albert Pujols' 130 in 2001.

Twitter: @KrisBryant_23

Did you know? Kris is engaged to his high school sweetheart, Jessica Delp, a standout softball and basketball player at Bonanza High in Las Vegas.

As a kid: Kris played on the same team, the Southern Nevada Bulldogs, as 2015 NL MVP Bryce Harper. Kris was 14 and Bryce 13.

Favorite foods: Kris loves Chicago's restaurant scene, particularly the steakhouses, as steak is his favorite. He also enjoys guilty pleasures like ice cream, chocolate, and sour candy or Junior Mints at the movies.

Fun fact: The Toronto Blue Jays drafted Kris in the 18th round of the 2010 draft, but he decided to attend the University of San Diego instead.

Fun fact: The toughest pitcher Kris has ever faced was Chris Sale, from the crosstown rival White Sox.

Favorite music: While he has a lot of Taylor Swift songs on his phone, his walk-up music is "Gone" by Donnis.

The No. 2 overall pick of the 2013 draft, Kris Bryant embodies the youth movement of the resurgent Chicago Cubs under Theo Epstein. In 2015 Bryant and fellow first-round picks Addison Russell, Kyle Schwarber, and Javier Baez showed why Cubs fans have reason to be hopeful (for once).

But it is Bryant who was and is the most complete player among the rookies who debuted in 2015, and it's why he was the unanimous choice for Rookie of the Year and made the All-Star team after only two months in the majors. In addition to playing a solid third base and filling in smoothly in the outfield (a flexibility highly valued by manager Joe Maddon), Bryant hit .275 with 26 home runs and 99 RBIs in his first season in the majors. He was an integral part of a team that won 97 games and made it deep into the playoffs for the first time since 2003.

Growing up in Las Vegas, at the age of 10 Bryant was already walloping 300-foot-long drives off of 13-year-old pitchers. In high school he was named first-team All-USA by *USA Today*. And in college he hit 31 homers as a junior in 2013, leading the nation and winning the Golden Spikes Award and Dick Howser Trophy as best collegiate player.

In 2013 Bryant was one of the hottest baseball prospects in the nation, and the Cubs were fortunate to get him at No. 2 when the Houston Astros went with pitcher Mark Appel at No. 1. Bryant excelled immediately in Class A, the Arizona Fall League, then Double A before being promoted to Triple A in June 2014. He was invited to spring training in 2015 and hit .425 with nine homers in just 40 at-bats. Only financial considerations kept him off the Opening Day roster, but by April 17, he was in the majors to stay.

On September 6, Bryant smashed a 495-foot home run high off the new video board in left at Wrigley Field, the longest clout in the majors in 2015. With 11 homers and 37 RBIs through 49 games in 2016, Bryant has picked up right where he left off.

"God has given him a tremendous left arm that can throw the ball very hard.... He also has very good touch and feel."

—White Sox pitching coach Don Cooper

Chris Sale

Hometown: Lakeland, Florida

Team: Chicago White Sox

Full name: Christopher Allen Sale

Ht: 6'6" • **Wt:** 180

DOB: March 30, 1989

Position: Pitcher

2016 Salary: $9,150,000

Bats/Throws: Left/Left

Fast stat: *9-0* — Chris' AL-leading record in his first nine starts of 2016.

Did you know? Chris is just one of five players in MLB history to play in the majors the same year he was drafted.

As a kid: When asked by his kindergarten teacher what he wanted to be when he grew up, Chris said "baseball player." Encouraging Chris' dream, his father built a pitching mound in their backyard.

Interesting tidbit: Prior to a college game attended by numerous scouts a month before the 2010 baseball draft, Chris got food poisoning from a bad cheeseburger, yet still managed to pitch a four-hit, seven-inning shutout.

Fun fact: Chris has finished in the top six in Cy Young Award voting each year from 2012 to 2015.

Fun fact: Chris was drafted No. 13 in the first round of the 2010 draft. In one of his first major league games, he struck out Joe Mauer on three pitches. Mauer remarked, "You mean to tell me there were 12 guys better than him?"

Favorite music: Chris' walk-up music is "Sail" by electronic rock band AWOLNATION.

Drafted in the first round by the Chicago White Sox in June 2010, Chris Sale was pitching in the majors just two months later. Called up to join the pitching staff as a reliever, the 21-year-old hurler went 2–1, posted a 1.93 ERA, and picked up four saves in 21 appearances. He continued to shine as a set-up man in 2011, going 2–2 with a 2.79 ERA and eight saves over 58 games.

In 2012 the White Sox moved Sale into the starting rotation, and he immediately became one of the top starters in the game. He made the first of four straight All-Star Games that season and finished with a 17–8 record and 3.05 ERA in 29 starts.

Nicknamed "the Condor" for his funky sidearm delivery and lanky 82-inch wingspan, Sale features a fastball that tops out at around 99 mph. Combined with a change-up and a hard-breaking slider, he's become one of the toughest strikeout artists in baseball, striking out more than 200 batters every year since 2013. In 2015 he led the American League with a White Sox franchise record 274 Ks.

On May 28, 2012, Sale struck out 15 batters against Tampa Bay in only seven-and-a-third innings in a 2–1 win, second best in Sox history. He pitched two innings of no-hit ball in the 2013 All-Star Game, earning a victory in the midsummer classic, which the AL won 3–0. That same year, Sale took a perfect game into the seventh inning against the Angels before allowing a single to Mike Trout, finishing the complete-game, one-hit shutout allowing only one base runner. In 2015 Sale tied Pedro Martinez' record of eight consecutive starts with at least 10 strikeouts.

In 2016 Sale took his game to another level, going 9–0 in his first nine starts with a 1.58 ERA, 0.717 WHIP (walks/hits per inning pitched), and a 6.2 strikeout-to-walk ratio. With Jake Arrieta on the North Side and Sale on the South Side, Chicago in 2016 boasts arguably the best pitcher in the National League and perhaps the best in the American League as well.

> "Hitting. Running. Defense. Throwing. He's got it all. You can't hit a ball [past him] out there. He's got lightning in that bat too."
> —former Atlanta Braves manager Bobby Cox

Andrew McCutchen

Hometown: Fort Meade, Florida

Full name:
Andrew Stefan McCutchen

Ht: 5'10" • **Wt:** 185

Team: Pittsburgh Pirates

DOB: October 10, 1986

Position: Center field

Salary: $13,000,000

Bats/Throws: Right/Right

Fast stat: *194* — Andrew led the National League in 2012 with 194 hits.

Twitter: @TheCUTCH22

Did you know? Andrew stole 20 or more bases in each of his first five major league seasons.

As a kid: Andrew was a star athlete in high school. In addition to baseball, he ran track and played football, becoming one of the top football prospects in Florida before committing to baseball.

Favorite foods: Andrew's favorite restaurant is Brazilian steakhouse chain Texas de Brazil, since they serve unlimited meat to diners.

Fun fact: Andrew's father was a talented college football player who gave up his dream of a pro career to be close to his son and become a Christian minister.

Fun fact: Andrew was part of a state title–winning 4×100-meter relay his freshman year of high school.

Favorite music: Andrew likes rap music, especially Lil Wayne.

One of the best all-around players in the major leagues for the last five years, Andrew McCutchen has been a key member of a Pittsburgh Pirates team that has made the postseason three years running. Anchoring center field, McCutchen hits for power and average, can steal bases, and plays exceptional defense. Winning the National League MVP award after leading the Pirates to a playoff berth in 2013, McCutchen has finished in the top five of MVP voting every year since 2012.

A home-grown prospect from the Pittsburgh system, McCutchen was a first-round draft choice in 2005. He earned his first call-up when the team traded starting center fielder Nate McLouth in 2009. He rewarded the team for their trust in his ability, singling in his first career at-bat. Within a week McCutchen had recorded a four-hit game and his time in the minors was over for good. Even though he'd missed the first two months of the season, the young center fielder finished his rookie year hitting .286 with 12 home runs, 54 RBIs, and 22 stolen bases.

A consistent run-producer and rangy center fielder, McCutchen quickly earned the respect of fans and opponents alike. A lifetime .296 hitter, he's hit more than 20 homers every year since 2011 and has made the All-Star team each of those seasons as well, winning a Gold Glove in 2012. In his MVP year of 2013, he hit .317 with 21 home runs and 84 RBIs, and stole 27 bases. Perhaps more important, he helped lead the Pirates to their first postseason appearance since 1992. Since then, Pittsburgh has been a perennial winner, and McCutchen is a huge reason why.

Prior to the 2015 season, McCutchen, who was known for his long dreadlocks, cut them off and put them up for auction through the MLB's website, the proceeds going to Pirates Charities. After another stellar year in 2015 with a .292 average, 23 homers, and 96 RBIs, he won the Roberto Clemente Award, given to the major leaguer who best exemplifies sportsmanship and community involvement.

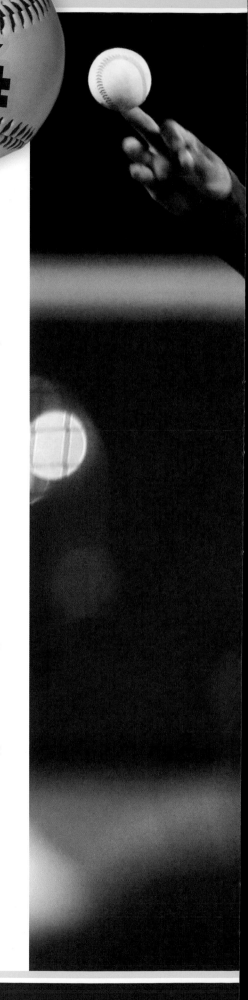

> *"When he's on, no pitcher in baseball is as nasty."*
> —*Bleacher Report* columnist Zachary D. Rymer

#34

Félix Hernández

Hometown: Valencia, Venezuela

Team: Seattle Mariners

Full name:
Félix Abraham Hernández Garcia

Ht: 6'3" • **Wt:** 225

DOB: April 8, 1986

Position: Pitcher

2016 Salary: $25,857,000

Bats/Throws: Right/Right

Fast stat: *2,189* — Career Ks by Félix, most in Mariners history (breaking the record held by Randy Johnson).

Twitter: @RealKingFelix

Did you know? In 2006 and 2007, Félix threw the fastest fastball of any starter in the majors, exceeding 95 mph on average.

As a kid: Félix was first spotted by a Mariners scout at age 14 in a tournament near Maracaibo, Venezuela.

Interesting tidbit: In 2011 a special cheering section for Félix, the "King's Court," debuted in Safeco Field in the left-field stands.

Fun fact: On June 23, 2008, Félix hit a grand slam in his only at-bat of the season—the first grand slam hit by an AL pitcher since the introduction of the designated hitter in 1973.

Fun fact: On June 17, 2008, Félix became the 13th AL pitcher ever to throw an "immaculate inning"—striking out the side on nine pitches.

Favorite music: Hip-hop, salsa, and merengue.

Able to throw 90 mph by the age of 14, Félix Hernández had remarkable stuff from early on. And it seems as he gets older, he just gets tougher to hit. Any time "King Félix" takes the mound, he's capable of no-hitting his opponents—as he did on August 23, 2012, when he pitched the first perfect game in Mariners history, a 1–0 win over the Tampa Bay Rays. It was only the 23rd perfect game ever thrown in major league history.

Hernández has been a Seattle Mariner since he was 16. Growing up in Venezuela, he idolized his countryman Freddy Garcia, a hurler for the Mariners. So when several major league teams—including the Yankees, Braves, and Astros—offered to sign him out of high school, he accepted a lower bid from the M's. As a 17-year-old minor leaguer, he tore through the competition in Class A ball and quickly moved up to Double A in 2004, Triple A in 2005, and the majors by August 2005.

As the top pitching prospect in the minors according to *Baseball America*, he did not disappoint once with the big-league club, despite being just 19 years old. In only his second start, on August 9, 2005, he pitched eight innings of shutout ball against the Minnesota Twins to earn his first major league win. He finished the season 4–4 but with a sparkling 2.67 ERA.

By 2007 the 21-year-old was named the team's Opening Day starter. He hurled his first one-hitter that season, a complete-game 3–0 victory over the Red Sox in Fenway Park.

Hernández had his best season yet in 2009, posting a 19–5 record and 2.49 ERA to go with 217 Ks, and was runner-up to Zack Greinke for the AL Cy Young Award. But in 2010 he won the Cy Young despite a 13–12 record, as he had an MLB-best 2.27 ERA and 232 Ks. He's complied a 147–104 career record with Seattle, despite playing on teams that have yet to make the playoffs. Off to a fast start in 2016, the Mariners hope King Félix can finally reign in October.

#27

> "When he was playing in low A ball, they were in awe of his raw power....What he wanted to do more than anything was... become a complete baseball player."
> —Marlins scouting director Stan Meek

Giancarlo Stanton

Hometown:
Panorama CIty, California

Team: Miami Marlins

Full name:
Giancarlo Cruz-Michael Stanton

Ht: 6'6" • **Wt:** 245

DOB: November 8, 1989

Position: Right field

2016 Salary: $9,000,000

Bats/Throws: Right/Right

Fast stat: *193* — Giancarlo's career home run total makes him the all-time leader for the Florida/Miami Marlins franchise.

Twitter: @Giancarlo818

Did you know? Prior to the 2012 season, Giancarlo was known as Mike Stanton.

As a kid: Giancarlo was a three-sport athlete at Notre Dame High School in Sherman Oaks, California.

Favorite foods: Steak and fried eggs, and grilled-cheese sandwiches.

Fun tidbit: Every October Giancarlo travels to Europe with teammate A.J. Ramos and pitcher Ricky Nolasco.

Fun fact: In November 2014, the Marlins signed Giancarlo to the richest contract in sports history, worth $325 million over 13 years.

Fun fact: Giancarlo has hit some of the longest home runs in the league since coming up in 2010—including clouts of 475 feet in 2011, 494 feet in 2012, and 472 feet in 2013.

Favorite music: Hip-hop, R&B.

Giancarlo Stanton made his major league debut with the Marlins on June 6, 2010, at the age of 20. He was the third youngest player in Marlins history after Édgar Rentería and Miguel Cabrera—not bad company. He'd shown prodigious power while tearing through every level of the minors and went 3-for-5 in his first game in the big leagues, scoring twice. But it was his first home run that was especially memorable—a grand slam off of the Tampa Bay Rays' Matt Garza. Stanton would finish his rookie season with 22 homers and 59 RBIs, and was named to *Baseball America*'s All-Rookie Team.

Although he battled injuries in 2011, Stanton still smashed 34 home runs while knocking in 87 runs. His 56 home runs before age 22 matched Alex Rodriguez and was behind only Ken Griffey Jr. in the last 40 years. Stanton would add another 37 in 2012 and be named to his first All-Star team (although injury would prevent him from playing). He posted a career-best .290 batting average and MLB-leading .608 slugging percentage, and also was named a Wilson Defensive Player of the Year for his play in right field.

A disappointing 2013 season saw Stanton miss two months with a hamstring injury. Even in limited action, though, he put up 22 more homers and 62 RBIs. But a healthier 2014 translated into Stanton's best all-around campaign. He led the National League in home runs (37), slugging (.555), and total bases (299), despite missing the last two weeks of the season after being hit in the face with a pitch. He made his second All-Star team that year—this time starting at DH—and finished second in National League MVP voting.

In 2015 injury again took its toll. A broken hand in late June caused him to miss the rest of the season after clubbing 27 homers in just 74 games. Despite slumping after returning in early 2016 with a low batting average, Stanton continues to hit home runs at a blistering pace. If he can manage to stay healthy, odds are his average will bounce back, and his power numbers could eventually be among the best ever.

"He wants to do things that help the team.... He's got it down. He's got a real maturity about his preparation."
—Baltimore Orioles manager Buck Showalter

#13

Manny Machado

Hometown: Miami, Florida

Team: Baltimore Orioles

Full name: Manuel Arturo Machado

Ht: 6'3" • **Wt:** 185

DOB: July 6, 1992

Position: Third base/Shortstop

2016 Salary: $5,000,000

Bats/Throws: Right/Right

Fast stat: *16* — Manny's career-best consecutive-game hitting streak to start the 2016 season. He hit .397 with six homers and 11 RBIs in that span.

Did you know? Manny's Gold Glove in 2013 was the first for any Orioles third baseman since Hall of Famer Brooks Robinson won it every year from 1960 to 1975.

As a kid: Manny was raised by his mother Rosa, grandmother, aunt, and uncle Gio Brito in inner-city Miami. His Uncle Gio coached him as a young baseball player.

Favorite foods: New York–style pizza and Philly cheesesteak.

Fun fact: Manny was the only major league player to appear in all 162 games in 2015.

Fun fact: In Manny's only two full seasons in the majors (2013 and 2015), he's won a Gold Glove for his defense at third base, been named to the All-Star team, and finished in the top 10 for AL MVP voting.

Favorite music: Manny's walk-up music is "Taxi" by Pit Bull.

A natural shortstop, Manny Machado has become the best fielding third baseman in baseball since coming up in 2012. Chosen third overall in the 2010 amateur draft by Baltimore, Machado is no slouch at the plate, either.

Showing real pop in his bat from the get-go, he was called up in August 2012 and became a fixture at third, hitting his first two homers in only his second game as a big-leaguer. The 19-year-old started all 51 games down the stretch, helping the Orioles to a wild-card berth, where Machado picked up his first postseason hit and first RBI in Baltimore's win over Texas. He then collected his first postseason home run in a losing effort to the New York Yankees in the ALDS.

Machado hit 14 home runs in his first full season in 2013, batting .283 with 71 RBIs and a league-leading 51 doubles. He was rewarded for his defense at third with his first Gold Glove and also won the Platinum Glove as the AL's best overall fielder at any position.

The 21-year-old infielder was cruising along to another strong season in 2014 when a knee injury took him out halfway through, after only 82 games. But in 2015 Machado managed to stay healthy (being the only major leaguer to play in all 162 games) and turned in his best all-around performance. Awarded a Gold Glove for the second time, he also improved his offense. Taking more than twice as many walks as he did in 2013, he improved his on-base percentage to a career-best .359, while also setting career marks for batting average (.286), homers (35), RBIs (86), stolen bases (20), slugging (.502), and total bases (318). He finished the season fifth in AL MVP voting.

Moving over to shortstop in May 2016 due to injury, Machado is off to the best start of his career, hitting safely in the first 16 games of the season and being named AL Player of the Month for April. By June 1, he was hitting .317 with 13 homers and was second in the majors in total bases with 124. With an Orioles team off to an equally strong start, Machado hopes to show off his talents in the playoffs once again.

> *"I wish we had 25 of him."*
> —Dodgers manager Dave Roberts

Clayton Kershaw

Hometown: Dallas, Texas

Team: Los Angeles Dodgers

Full name: Clayton Edward Kershaw

Ht: 6'4" · **Wt:** 225

DOB: March 19, 1988

Position: Pitcher

2016 Salary: $34,571,429

Bats/Throws: Left/Left

Fast stat: *2.39* — Clayton's lifetime ERA is the lowest of any starter since the dead-ball era ended in 1920.

Twitter: @ClaytonKersh22

Did you know? Clayton's first Cy Young Award in 2011 made him the youngest recipient of the award since Dwight Gooden in 1985.

As a kid: Clayton attended Highland Park High School in Texas, where he played baseball and also was the center for future NFL quarterback Matthew Stafford on the varsity football team.

Fun tidbit: He idolized Will Clark as a kid, which is why he wears No. 22.

Fun fact: Since 2011 Clayton has finished in the top three in voting for the Cy Young Award every year, winning it three times.

Fun fact: Clayton and his wife, Ellen, started "Kershaw's Challenge" to help raise money to build an orphanage in Zambia. For his humanitarian work, he has been honored with the Roberto Clemente Award and the Branch Rickey Award.

Favorite music: Taylor Swift and the Red Hot Chili Peppers.

If there's any pitcher on the planet worth $34 million a year, it's the Dodgers' three-time Cy Young Award winner/one-time MVP Clayton Kershaw. In just seven full seasons in Los Angeles, the hard-throwing left-hander has led the majors in ERA an astounding four times. His *lifetime* ERA, with more than 1,690 innings pitched in 254 games, is a measly 2.39. He's won 20-plus games in a season twice, led the league in strikeouts three times, and has a career record of 121–57 (a .680 winning percentage).

Kershaw was taken seventh by the Dodgers in the 2006 draft, working his way up to the big-league club in just one season, debuting in 2008 as the youngest player then in the majors at 20 years old. In his highly anticipated debut on May 25, he struck out seven and gave up two runs over six innings in a no-decision. He would go on to a decent rookie year, posting a 5–5 record with an unspectacular 4.26 ERA. It would be the last season he didn't finish with an ERA under 3.00. From his first full season in 2009, he has dominated National League hitters, putting up sub-3.00 ERAs every year—sub-2.00 ERAs twice.

In 2011 he won his first Cy Young Award after leading the league in wins (21), ERA (2.28), and strikeouts (248). In 2013 he won his second Cy Young, posting a 16–9 record with a league-leading 1.83 ERA and 232 strikeouts. In 2014 he went 21–3 with a 1.77 ERA and 239 strikeouts. He led the majors in wins, winning percentage, ERA, complete games, and WHIP, and on June 18 pitched a no-hitter against Colorado, striking out 15 (a career high) and walking none (an error prevented it being a perfect game). At the end of the season, he won his third Cy Young Award and first MVP.

In 2015 Kershaw had a career-high 301 Ks and finished third in Cy Young voting. The five-time All-Star, who had struggled in the playoffs, pitched well in the NLDS, going 1–1 with a 2.63 ERA and clutch Game 4 victory in a 3–2 series loss to the Mets. With a 7–1 record, 1.56 ERA, and ridiculous 21:1 strikeout-to-walk ratio as of June 1, 2016, Kershaw remains in a class by himself.

"He is loved by everyone, respected by all... one of the most prolific clutch hitters in the history of the game. He has been the centerpiece of three world championships."

—Yankees All-Star Alex Rodriguez

David Ortiz

Hometown:
Santo Domingo, Dominican Republic

Team: Boston Red Sox

Full name:
David Américo Ortiz Arias

Ht: 6'3" • **Wt:** 230

DOB: November 18, 1975

Position: Designated hitter

Salary: $16,000,000

Bats/Throws: Left/Left

Fast stat: *54* — Ortiz holds the Red Sox single-season home run record after he belted 54 homers in 2006.

Twitter: @davidortiz

Did you know? David's 607 career doubles is the most of any active player.

As a kid: David's easy smile was his trademark growing up in the Dominican Republic. The oldest of four kids, he was easygoing and known in his family for his sense of humor.

Interesting tidbit: David's wife is from Wisconsin, and he has become an avid fan of the Green Bay Packers over the years.

Fun fact: David hit .688 with two homers and six RBIs on his way to being named MVP of the 2013 World Series vs. the St. Louis Cardinals.

Favorite music: David enjoys reggaeton music and has recorded songs and made music videos.

One of the best clutch hitters in baseball history, the man known affectionately as "Big Papi" remains one of the most popular players as well. A rotund slugger with an easy smile and a playfulness that reflects a true love of the game, David Ortiz is one of the greatest hitters of his era. He has been there in big moments for his Boston Red Sox time after time, bashing many memorable home runs and clutch hits as the team gained a place among the game's elite with three World Series titles in 10 years.

A nine-time All-Star, Ortiz began his career with the Minnesota Twins. Though he showed potential and the Twins knew he could become an elite hitter, injuries forced his release. Signing with the Boston Red Sox in 2003 rejuvenated his career and sent him down a sure Hall of Fame path that will reach its completion at the end of the 2016 season, which the 40-year-old Ortiz says will be his last.

Ortiz broke out in his first year in Boston, collecting 31 homers and 101 RBIs as the Red Sox made it to within one game of a World Series berth. The next year, Ortiz was a major part of the Red Sox team that broke the famed "Curse of the Bambino" and won the World Series for the first time since 1918. After a huge regular season, Ortiz hit a walk-off home run to win the Division Series and followed that up with another walk-off homer as the Sox held off elimination in Game 4 of the ALCS against the Yankees. He delivered another walk-off hit in the next game, giving the Sox all the momentum they needed to make their historic comeback from being down three games to none.

World Series titles followed in 2007 and again in 2013, for which Ortiz was named Series MVP. With 517 career home runs and 1,688 RBIs, he is 22nd and 27th all-time, respectively. Through the first two months of his farewell season of 2016, Big Papi is leading his first-place Red Sox with what could be the best season of his illustrious career, hitting .335 with 14 homers, while leading the majors with 47 RBIs, a .716 slugging percentage, and 126 total bases.

> *"[I'm] a big fan of his....Seeing a guy like that brings back a lot of great memories."*
> —Mets pitching great Dwight "Doc" Gooden

#33

Matt Harvey

Hometown: Mystic, Connecticut

Team: New York Mets

Full name: Matthew Edward Harvey

Ht: 6'4" • **Wt:** 215

DOB: March 27, 1989

Position: Pitcher

2016 Salary: $4,325,000

Bats/Throws: Right/Right

Fast stat: 9.2 — Matt's lifetime strikeouts-per-nine-innings ratio.

Twitter: @MattHarvey33

Did you know? Matt was the 2015 Comeback Player of the Year.

As a kid: Matt actually grew up in Connecticut as a New York Yankees fan, idolizing Derek Jeter.

Interesting tidbit: Matt appeared nude in "The Body Issue" of *ESPN The Magazine* in 2013.

Fun fact: A Batman fan since childhood, Matt had his nickname, "Dark Knight," carved into the knobs of his bats in early 2015 before replacing that with his own Harvey-Batman logo.

Fun fact: Matt is a passionate New York Rangers hockey fan.

Favorite music: Matt's regular walk-up music is "Sunday Bloody Sunday" by U2.

Chosen by the New York Mets with the seventh overall pick in the 2010 draft, Matt Harvey had one of the most anticipated debuts of any Met in recent memory. Called up in late July 2012 to a Mets team that was going nowhere, the hard-throwing, 6'4" right-hander fanned 70 batters in 59⅓ innings, posting an impressive 2.73 ERA, and giving fans hope for a bright future.

In 2013 Harvey upped his game and got off to a sizzling start, named National League Pitcher of the Month for April after putting up a 1.56 ERA and striking out 46 batters in 40⅓ innings. He was the hottest pitcher in the National League and was named the starting pitcher for the NL in the All-Star Game in July.

After being featured on the May 20, 2013, issue of *Sports Illustrated*, which dubbed him "The Dark Knight of Gotham," Mets fans adopted the nickname. They also started referring to each start by the All-Star as "Harvey Day," as he continued to dominate opposing teams. On August 7, he pitched his first complete-game shutout, a 5–0 victory over the Colorado Rockies. But in late August, after logging over 178 innings, Harvey was diagnosed with a tear of the ulnar collateral ligament in his pitching elbow. Forced to undergo Tommy John surgery, Harvey missed all of 2014 while he underwent rehab. It was an open question how effective he would be in his return and to what extent he would be able to pitch.

By 2015 Harvey rejoined a team that now contended and a rotation with 2014 Rookie of the Year Jacob deGrom and 2015 rookie sensation Noah Syndergaard. With his surgically repaired arm, Harvey led the Mets into the postseason and past both the Dodgers and Cubs on their way to a World Series berth versus the Kansas City Royals. Despite coming off the year-long rehab, Harvey was a workhorse, throwing 216 innings including the postseason. He went 13–8 with a 2.71 ERA in the regular season and 2–0 with a 3.04 ERA in a postseason that ended with the Mets falling to the Royals in the World Series, four games to one.

> *"There's not a pitch you can throw him that he can't do damage with. In my eyes, he's the best hitter in the game."*
> — Detroit Tigers pitcher Jordan Zimmermann

Miguel Cabrera

Hometown: Maracay, Venezuela

Team: Detroit Tigers

Full name:
José Miguel Cabrera Torres

Ht: 6'4" • **Wt:** 240

DOB: April 18, 1983

Position: First base

Salary: $28,000,000

Bats/Throws: Right/Right

Fast stat: .330/44/139 — Miguel's Triple Crown–winning batting average, home runs, and RBIs.

Twitter: @MiguelCabrera

Did you know? With 1,476, Miguel has more RBIs than any Venezuelan player in major league history.

As a kid: Miguel's backyard bordered Maracay's baseball stadium, where he hopped the fence to watch games.

Interesting tidbit: Miguel's parents met at a baseball field. His dad was an excellent amateur player and his mom played softball for Venezuela's national team for 14 years.

Fun fact: Miguel drove in at least 100 runs for 11 straight years, from 2004 to 2014.

Fun fact: Miguel was just 20 when he entered the major leagues; he has been considered an MVP-caliber player since his debut and won the AL MVP award twice (2012 and 2013).

Favorite music: Miguel enjoys hip-hop. His walk-up music is currently "Hypnotize" by Notorious B.I.G.

The first Triple Crown winner in baseball since 1967, two-time MVP Miguel Cabrera has been the best hitter in baseball over the last 12 years. A 10-time All-Star and four-time batting champion, Cabrera plays solid defense at first base and hits the ball all over the field when he's at the plate.

Only 20 years old when he made his big-league debut with Florida in 2003, Cabrera immediately established himself in the major leagues by hitting a walk-off home run in his first game. The Marlins used Cabrera as their cleanup hitter, riding their hot rookie all the way to a World Series championship.

Cabrera showed that his strong rookie campaign was no fluke, returning to the Marlins to hit 33 home runs and drive in 112 on a depleted team. He made his first All-Star appearance that year and was already known as one of the most dangerous hitters in the game. After making four straight All-Star appearances with the Marlins, he was traded to the Detroit Tigers and signed an eight-year deal with the team.

He entered the American League in 2008 with a bang, belting a league-best 37 homers in his first season in Detroit. He made his fifth All-Star Game in 2010, the first of six straight, and continued to hit for power and average. If any player was going to win the first Triple Crown since Carl Yastrzemski did it in 1967, it was going to be Cabrera. In 2012 he went on a tear, yet it still took him until the last day of the season to clinch the Triple Crown. His .330 average, 44 home runs, and 139 RBIs secured Cabrera's place as one of the best hitters of all-time. Incredibly, though he didn't repeat the feat in 2013, his numbers were just as good as they were in 2012 (.348/44 HRs/137 RBIs).

Cabrera has also excelled in the postseason, hitting 13 homers and driving in 38 runs in 55 games, though his only World Series title came in his rookie year. He won another batting title in 2015 despite missing six weeks during his only trip to the disabled list in his career. Now in his 14th season, Cabrera is once again among the league leaders in average, home runs, and RBIs.

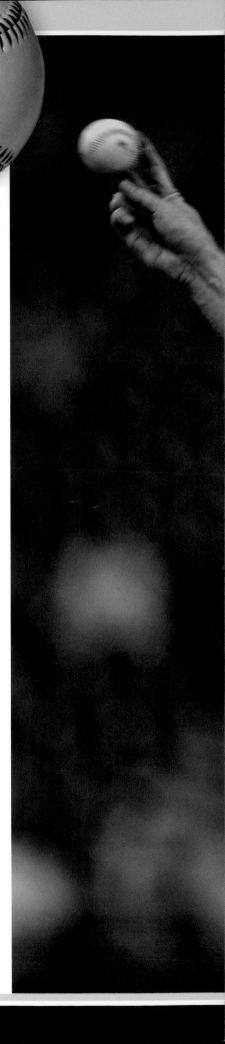

> *"It's awesome. It's fun to watch…. [It can] be boring at times because he strikes everybody out."*
> —Nationals third baseman Anthony Rendon

#37

Stephen Strasburg

Hometown: San Diego, California

Team: Washington Nationals

Full name: Stephen James Strasburg

Ht: 6'4" • **Wt:** 235

DOB: July 20, 1988

Position: Pitcher

Salary: $10,400,000

Bats/Throws: Right/Right

Fast stat: *14* — Stephen struck out 14 batters in his major league debut, setting a franchise record.

Twitter: @stras37

Did you know? Stephen's 2012 season ended at 15 wins when he reached an innings limit placed on him before the season by the team. When the Nationals made the playoffs, they continued to rest Strasburg for 2013.

As a kid: Stephen played baseball in high school but struggled at times, including a 1–10 record as a junior.

Interesting tidbit: Stephen pitched on Team USA with Jake Arrieta in the 2008 Summer Olympics, going 1–1 and helping the United States win the bronze medal.

Fun fact: If his career ended today, Strasburg would have the second best strikeouts-per-nine-innings ratio (10.5) of all-time.

Fun fact: No pitcher struck out 100 batters in 2012 In a shorter amount of time than Strasburg.

Favorite music: Stephen likes country music, especially the Zac Brown Band.

Stephen Strasburg first became a prospect while playing for Hall of Famer Tony Gwynn at San Diego State University. Though he battled with his weight early in his college career, Strasburg disciplined himself and became a better pitcher every day, quickly turning himself into a big-time talent. His status was solidified when he became the only college player named to the 2008 U.S. Olympic team that took the bronze in Beijing.

Selected first overall in the 2009 draft, Strasburg was fast-tracked through the Nationals system. He earned his first call-up in June 2010 and set the baseball world on fire in his debut. Called "the most hyped pitching debut the game has ever seen" by *Sports Illustrated*, Strasburg struck out 14 over seven innings, walking none and earning the win. The hype matched the ability. Strasburg's rookie season was cut short in August, however, after just 12 starts. He needed Tommy John surgery on his elbow and was out for a year. Still, he had proven that he had the skills to be an ace in the majors.

After returning from his injury in September 2011, Strasburg was ready to hit the ground running in 2012. Though his season was cut short by an innings limit imposed by the team, the young hurler still won 15 games for a Nationals club that finished with the best record in baseball. Strasburg was named to his first All-Star team but was forced to sit out the playoffs.

Strasburg put together a solid 2013, pitching the first complete-game shutout of his career and posting a 3.00 ERA, but with a modest 8–9 record. In 2014 he showed the form that made him the most hyped pitcher in baseball, leading the league in strikeouts with 242 and winning 14 games, helping his Nationals to another division title. This time he played in the NLDS but lost his only start in the Nationals' 3–1 series loss to the Giants. Although he took a step back in the first half of 2015, he finished the year strong.

In 2016 Strasburg is off to the best start of his career, going 9–0 with a 2.69 ERA in his first 11 starts.

43

#50

> *"He's got that swag. He's got what the game needs right now....You just have to let that kid play and enjoy."*
> — Red Sox All-Star DH David Ortiz

Mookie Betts

Hometown: Brentwood, Tennessee

Team: Boston Red Sox

Full name: Markus Lynn Betts

Ht: 5'9" • **Wt:** 180

DOB: October 7, 1992

Position: Right field

2016 Salary: $566,000

Bats/Throws: Right/Right

Fast stat: .581 — Mookie's batting average June 15–21, 2015, when he was named American League Player of the Week. He also had two homers, two triples, three double, eight runs, and seven RBIs.

Twitter: @mookiebetts

Did you know? Mookie's parents named him so that his initials would be "MLB" (Major League Baseball). The nickname "Mookie" actually comes from NBA guard Mookie Blaylock.

As a kid: Mookie's first coach in little league was his mother, Diana.

Interesting tidbit: Mookie has been with his fiancée, Brianna, since middle school.

Fun fact: A talented bowler who's bowled two sanctioned 300 games, Mookie was named the 2010 Tennessee boys Bowler of the Year in high school, and in December 2015 he competed in the PBA World Series of Bowling in Reno, Nevada.

Fun fact: Mookie's favorite TV show is *SpongeBob SquarePants*.

Favorite music: Mookie likes hip-hop but admits to having a few country songs on his playlist.

Red Sox fans of a certain age probably wouldn't believe they'd be rooting for any player named Mookie—not after the Mets' Mookie Wilson hit the grounder that dribbled through Bill Buckner's legs in Game 6 of the 1986 World Series. But Red Sox right fielder Mookie Betts has quickly become a fan favorite for his infectious energy and enthusiasm, whether it's for robbing an opposing batter of a home run, hitting one of his many triples, or stealing second and third base in quick succession.

A speedy 5'9" middle infielder and outfielder, Betts was a fifth-round draft choice of the Red Sox in 2011. Moving up through the minors, Betts started the 2014 season in Double A but was called up to the majors in June, where he shuttled back and forth between Boston and Triple A affiliate Pawtucket. On August 29, he hit his first career grand slam in a Red Sox victory against the Rays in Tampa. Just 21, Betts was the youngest Sox player to hit a grand slam in 49 years. In 52 games with the Red Sox, split between center field, right field, and second base, Betts batted .291 with five homers and seven stolen bases.

By 2015 Betts was with the big-league club to stay, playing 145 games as Boston's regular center fielder. He hit a home run on Opening Day and, a week later in the Sox' home opener, hit another homer and made a leaping catch in center field to rob Bryce Harper of a home run. For the week ending June 21, Betts was named AL Player of the Week. In his first full season, he again batted .291, adding 18 home runs, 77 RBIs, 92 runs scored, and 21 stolen bases. He finished 19th in MVP voting for a last-place team and, if not for exceeding rookie limits in 2014, would have been a shoo-in for Rookie of the Year honors.

Moving to right field in 2016 to make room for center fielder Jackie Bradley Jr., Betts is once again thrilling fans as part of the most dangerous lineup in baseball. He's increased his power numbers to 12 homers and 40 RBIs as of June 1, including a three-home-run, five-RBI performance on May 31 versus the Baltimore Orioles.

#28

Buster Posey

Hometown: Leesburg, Georgia

Team: San Francisco Giants

Full name: Gerald Dempsey Posey III

Ht: 6'1" • **Wt:** 215

DOB: March 27, 1987

Position: Catcher/First base

Salary: $20,000,000

Bats/Throws: Right/Right

Fast stat: *.336* — Buster led the National League in 2012 with a .336 batting average.

Twitter: @BusterPosey

Did you know? Buster has caught three no-hitters for the Giants, one behind the record shared by Carlos Ruiz and Jason Varitek. He also played first base in Tim Lincecum's second career no-no.

As a kid: Buster's nickname actually comes from his dad, who was also called Buster as a kid.

Interesting tidbit: Shortstop is Buster's natural position. He switched to catcher in college because his team needed him to.

Fun fact: Buster's first two full major league seasons both ended with him catching the third strike of a World Series win for the Giants.

Fun fact: Buster was named the 2012 National League Comeback Player of the Year for his dramatic recovery from a career-threatening leg injury he suffered in 2011.

Favorite music: Buster enjoys country music and some rap.

One of the best defensive catchers in the majors over his seven-year career, Buster Posey is also one of the most dangerous hitters in the game, leading his San Francisco Giants to three World Series championships since his rookie year.

Drafted with the No. 5 pick in the first round of the 2008 draft, Posey, after seeing limited action with the big-league club in September 2009, was called up to the majors two months into the 2010 season. This time Posey left no doubt that he belonged in the big leagues. The National League Rookie of the Year, despite appearing in just 108 games, Posey took less than a year to establish himself as one of the game's best catchers. He hit 18 homers and drove in 67 runs but was at his best in the playoffs. He batted .300 in the World Series, beating the Texas Rangers four games to one and earning the Giants a title for the first time since moving to the West Coast in 1958.

Posey's 2011 was cut short just 45 games in after a collision at home plate left him with a broken leg and torn ligaments. The injury threatened a promising young career, and Posey missed the rest of the season. He returned in 2012 with a vengeance, however, winning the batting title with a .336 average, belting 24 homers, knocking in 103 runs, and leading his Giants back to the postseason. He was named to the All-Star team and won the NL MVP award but wasn't done there. Once again, he excelled in the playoffs, putting an exclamation point on his recovery as he hit a two-run homer in the decisive Game 4 of the World Series against the Detroit Tigers.

In 2014 he once again led his team to the promised land, helping the Giants to victory in a grueling seven-game World Series against the Kansas City Royals.

A lifetime .309 hitter, Posey has collected more than 100 home runs and 470 RBIs in a little over five full seasons in the majors. A three-time All-Star, he was named a Wilson Defensive Player of the Year at catcher in 2015. He also hit .318 with 19 homers and 95 RBIs in 2015 and is off to another hot start in 2016.

47

*The Dodgers' Clayton Kershaw delivers
to the Angels' Mike Trout*